The outside of a museum can be as interesting as the inside

Museums

Joanne Mattern

A⁺

Smart Apple Media

COPYRIGHT

❖ Published by Smart Apple Media

1980 Lookout Drive, North Mankato, MN 56003

Designed by Rita Marshall

Copyright © 2003 Smart Apple Media. International copyright reserved in all countries. No part of this book may be reproduced in any form without written permission from the publisher.

Printed in the United States of America

❖ Photographs by Richard Cummins, The Image Finders (Patti McConville), Sally McCrae Kuyper, Witold Skrypczak, Tom Stack & Associates (Brian Parker)

❖ Library of Congress Cataloging-in-Publication Data

Mattern, Joanne, 1963- Museums / by Joanne Mattern. p. cm. — (Structures)

Includes bibliographical references and index.

Summary: Discusses the purpose and special collections of different kinds of museums, what goes on behind the scenes, and how to start your own museum.

❖ ISBN 1-58340-149-0

1. Museums—Juvenile literature. [1. Museums.] I. Title. II. Structures

(North Mankato, Minn.)

AM5 .M38 2002   069—dc21   2001049971

❖ First Edition 9 8 7 6 5 4 3 2 1

Museums

CONTENTS

The First Museums

Where would you go if you wanted to hunt for treasure? How about visiting a museum? Museums are filled with **collections** of priceless and unusual treasures that people can look at and study. The English word "museum" comes from the ancient Greek word *mouseion*. The first museums were built in Greece. They were filled with books and artwork. ❖ During the 1400s and 1500s, European explorers traveled all over the world. They brought back

Many museums are specially designed for their collections

interesting animals, plants, and art objects. But only important people such as kings and queens were allowed to see these exhibits. ❖ In 1683, one of the world's first public museums opened. It was the Ashmolean in Oxford, England. The Ashmolean was named after Elias Ashmole. He filled the museum with a collection of unusual objects from faraway lands. Huge crowds of people came to see his discoveries.

In 1773, the Charleston Library Society in South Carolina opened the first museum in the United States.

The Louvre in Paris mixes old and new building styles

Buildings of Wonder

Today, museums are filled with colorful paintings, **sculptures**, and artifacts. But many museums are just as famous for what's *outside* as for what's inside. The Experience

Some museums have to be very large

Music Project in Seattle, Washington, was built to look like a pile of broken guitars. It displays one of Elvis Presley's leather jackets. The Louvre in Paris, France, has many buildings and courtyards. They are fine examples of different French building styles. ❖ When the Smithsonian Institution first opened in Washington, D.C., it was housed in a castle. In 1858, it became the National Museum of the United States. The Smithsonian now has 140 million artifacts in 16 museums! ❖ New York City's Guggenheim

New York's Sea and Air Museum is housed on a big ship called the *U.S.S. Intrepid*. It is docked on the Hudson River.

Museum is shaped like a spiral. Visitors take an elevator to the

top of the museum and walk down a curving ramp, viewing

works of art as they go. The museum exit is at the end of the

The oldest Smithsonian museum is called "the Castle"

ramp. The Guggenheim Museum has been called a "museum-go-round" because of its structure. ❖ Skansen, located in Stockholm, Sweden, was the world's first open-air museum. It was founded in 1891 and is still open today. Visitors to Skansen explore a historic village of 150 buildings, including huts, a mansion, stores, and workshops. The village is brought to life by actors in costumes who play the parts of silversmiths, farmers, shopkeepers, and other villagers. This kind of museum is also called a living history museum.

Treasures Galore

What will you find inside a museum? It depends

upon a museum's size, how much money it has, and what type

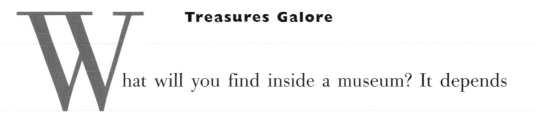

The Guggenheim Museum is itself a work of art

it is. Many museums are filled with fine art. The Louvre has 300,000 famous artworks, including the Mona Lisa. ❖ Some history museums have stone tools, jewelry, toys, or animal bones. The Field Museum of Natural History in Chicago, Illinois, recently acquired a dinosaur skeleton named Sue. She is the world's most complete tyrannosaurus rex. ❖ The **archaeology** museum at Simon Fraser University in British Columbia, Canada, has clay pots, jugs, and whistles from South America. Visitors to New York's

Curators are people who are in charge of museum collections. They decide how to obtain and display new objects.

Museum of the American Indian, Heye Center, view artifacts

from a Native American village in Georgia. ❖ Science

museums often teach visitors how things work, such as

This exhibit is about the history of transportation

machines or electricity. Visitors are invited to touch many of these exhibits. An exhibit at the Science Museum of Minnesota in St. Paul focused on the smelly, slimy things that come out of people's bodies. The exhibit was called *Grossology*.

Ready, Set, Explore!

Many museums focus on one thing. The Circus World Museum in Baraboo, Wisconsin, has a collection of circus wagons. The Asphalt Museum, located in California, displays a collection of blacktop pieces from famous highways. The National Baseball Hall of Fame in Cooperstown, New

York, is all about baseball. It has uniforms, equipment, and

information about great baseball players and old ballparks.

Some well-known people's houses are museums too. That is

Totem poles are on display at this archaeology museum

true of Thomas Jefferson's home in Monticello, Virginia. ❖

No matter what a person's interest is, there is probably a

museum to tell him or her more about it. Many museums

offer online "galleries" that you can **In the small town of Hayward, Wisconsin, a lumberjack museum shows how log cutters once lived and worked in the area.**

explore by computer from your home

or school. Some special museums

exist only online. Other museums

travel from place to place. With so many choices, why not visit

a museum today?

> **Thomas Jefferson's house is preserved as a museum**

Start Your Own Museum

Theodore Roosevelt was the 26th president of the United States. When he was a child, he started his own museum by collecting animal skeletons. You can start your own museum collection too!

What You Need

Objects you think are interesting, such as rocks, seashells, feathers, marbles, drawings, or ticket stubs
An empty egg carton
Tape
A pen
Paper

What You Do

1. Prop the egg carton open and number each section from 1 to 12.
2. Separate your objects into each section. Tape paper items (such as drawings) to the inside cover. Label those items A, B, C, and so on (write next to the item, not on it).
3. On a sheet of paper, write down the number or letter of each object, what it is, where you found it, and why you like it.
4. Open your museum for visitors!

Some museum objects are displayed outside the museum

INFORMATION

Index

Words to Know

acquired (uh-KWIRED)—added or gained

archaeology (ar-kee-AH-lah-jee)—the study of old cities and people

artifacts (AR-tuh-fax)—objects made or used by people

collections (kuh-LEK-shunz)—groups of things that have been gathered together in one place

exhibits (eg-ZIB-its)—public displays of collections and objects

sculptures (SKUHLP-churz)—works of art made of stone, wood, metal, or clay

Read More

Bay, Ann Phillips. *A Kid's Guide to the Smithsonian*. Washington, D.C.: Smithsonian Institution Press, 1996.

Brown, Laurene Krasny, and Marc Brown. *Visiting the Art Museum*. New York: NAL, 1990.

Relf, Pat, with the Sue Science Team of the Field Museum. *A Dinosaur Named Sue*. New York: Scholastic, 2000.

Internet Sites

The Museum of Archaeology and Ethnology, Simon Fraser University
http://www.sfu.ca/archaeology/museum/kids.html

Museum of Science and Industry, Chicago
http://www.msichicago.org

Smithsonian Institution
http://www.si.edu